AF413604

To Know Reality, We Need to Be Real

The Transformative Wisdom
of Breema

Also from The Breema Center

BOOKS:

Breema and the Nine Principles of Harmony

Knowing and Being: Breema and the Meaning of Your Life

Your Home Is the Entire Cosmos: The Wisdom of Breema

Real Health Means Harmony with Existence:
The Art of Practicing Breema

First You Have to Be:
The Nine Principles of Harmony in Breema and Life

The Taste of Being Present: Essential Wisdom of Breema

Child of Existence, Child of Society

Waking Up to This Moment: The Essential Meaning of Breema

The Four Relationships and Other Essential Insights

Coming to Yourself: The Art of Practicing Breema

In the Garden of All Possibilities: Essential Poetry

In the Heart of the Moment: Essential Poetry

Freedom Is in This Moment: 365 Insights for Daily Life

Every Moment Is Eternal: The Timeless Wisdom of Breema

Freedom Comes from Understanding: Insights for Meaningful Life

Seeing Things As They Really Are

Walking into the Sun: Stories from Classes at the Breema Center

AUDIO CDs:

Please see our website and the back pages of this book for audio CDs
of Breema Center books.

eBOOKS:

Download Breema eBooks from your favorite online book source.

TRANSLATIONS:

Despertando a este momento: el significado esencial de Breema

Selbst-Breema: Übungen für ein harmonisches Leben

Breema und die neun Prinzipien der Harmonie

To Know Reality, We Need to Be Real

The Transformative Wisdom of Breema

by Jon Schreiber

The Breema Center
Oakland, California

The Breema Center
6076 Claremont Avenue
Oakland, CA 94618

phone: 510.428.0937
email: center@breema.com
website: www.breema.com

To Know Reality, We Need to Be Real:
The Transformative Wisdom of Breema

Library of Congress Control Number: 2024923416
ISBN: 979-8-9858375-3-7 (print)
ISBN: 979-8-9858375-4-4 (ebook)

Front and back jacket photographs: Juancat and Galumphing Galah, courtesy of Shutterstock

eBook formatting by: Luminare Press

At some point in our life, we may become grateful for all the challenges life presents us with, because we know we can use them to purify ourselves and gain a little more inner strength. We wish to realize our potential to be in harmony with the totality of everything that exists.

Introduction

Many of the essays, sayings, and stories in this book are no more than a few words or sentences. But each one is like a ripe fruit hanging on the branch, inviting you to pick and eat it. When you do, you get a taste of *understanding* that could grow to eventually illuminate the entire universe for you!

What is it that makes Breema's philosophy so powerful? How is it that these writings, like mirrors, show us the emptiness of what we take ourselves to be, yet at the same time, allow us to look at ourselves with an accepting attitude that brings us fresh strength and clarity?

Personally, I have never encountered another Teaching that enables us to see ourselves in such sharp focus, yet with so much understanding and compassion that, instead of suffering, we become grateful for what we see.

The perspective that Breema reveals and makes available to us allows us to approach our life with a calm simplicity that is, at the same time, deeply fulfilling.

The underlying message of Breema offers us a realistic hope that can always support us. In spite of the difficulties of life on planet Earth, we each have a connection to Existence that cannot be broken, and by developing the ability to become and remain connected to our Timeless nature as we live our life in time, we can find meaning and purpose—and experience harmony and true fulfillment.

The material in this book comes from classes taught at the Breema Center, where I have had the good fortune to be a student since 1980. I hope it will nourish your heart and mind as much as it has mine. If these writings strike a resonant chord in you, you owe it to yourself to experience Breema as a recipient, or as a student. Even one direct experience of body-mind connection in a class can connect you to the harmony that is the organizing principle of the universe.

—Jon Schreiber

To Know Reality, We Need to Be Real

The Transformative Wisdom of Breema

BREEMA
The Nine Principles of Harmony

BODY COMFORTABLE

*When we look at the body, not as something separate,
but as an aspect of a unified whole, there is no
place for discomfort.*

NO EXTRA

To express our True nature, nothing extra is needed.

FIRMNESS AND GENTLENESS

*Real firmness is always gentle.
Real gentleness is always firm.
When we are present, we naturally
manifest firmness and gentleness simultaneously.*

FULL PARTICIPATION

*The most natural way of moving and living is with full
participation. Full participation is possible when body,
mind, and feelings are united in a common aim.*

MUTUAL SUPPORT

*The more our Being participates, the more we are able to
support life and recognize that Existence supports us.
Giving and receiving support take place simultaneously.*

NO JUDGMENT

*The atmosphere of nonjudgment gives us a taste of
acceptance of ourselves as we are in the moment. When
we come to the present, we are free from judgment.*

SINGLE MOMENT/SINGLE ACTIVITY

*Each moment is new, fresh, totally alive. Each moment
is an expression of our True nature, complete by itself.*

NO HURRY/NO PAUSE

*In the natural rhythm of life energy,
there is no hurry and no pause.*

NO FORCE

*When we let go of assumptions of separation,
we let go of force.*

Allow yourself the joy of being present, as if everything in the universe is exactly as it should be. Accept the way you are in this moment. Be grateful to be alive. Take a break from your concerns, from your problems with yourself and the world. Your problems are ripples on the surface of the ocean. But the ocean is still there. The ripples are temporary. They come and go.

There is one unified Existence. Be in it, and appreciate the sense of belonging. There is no extra. And even if there was, as soon as you accept it, it's no longer extra. Everything is subject to the law of constant change, yet everything also has an unchangeable aspect. Whatever isn't right is just a temporary manifestation of something that is always right. The sooner you come to acceptance, the sooner you can remain undisturbed in the midst of all disturbances. That which Existence has given you cannot be taken away by anyone or by any condition. Our reality is eternal, everlasting, always and everywhere. When you are present, you can taste that presence, and you and reality are not two different things.

When you bring mind, body, and feelings together, you are not affected by thoughts about the past. You let go of negativity. When they are together, they invite Consciousness. Consciousness is a light, and when it's there, the darkness of negativity disappears. Consciousness changes the way you look at things, the way you think, and the way you feel. It brings you to the bigger picture, where you can see how small your problems really are.

There is always something simple you can do to come to the world of meaning. Because the meaning is always there.

Ultimately, you have to see that when you say "I exist," you are saying "Existence exists in the form of I." When you know *there is a body,* it really means Existence exists in the form of this body. To exist means to be at the presence of Existence. That's being alive—anything other than that isn't!

15

What does it mean to taste your existence in the moment? You can't really define or describe it. But you can experience it. The closest you can come is to say "*I am.*" In that taste, everything that exists is you. You are the totality of past, present, and future. You are the meaning itself.

If you think everything is Existence, you have correct theoretical knowledge. But it's not really knowledge—it's a thought, and thought means assumption.

But if you know everything is Existence, and at the same time you have a taste of *body breathes*, a taste of *there is a body*, or of *I exist*, then your knowledge of Existence can be trusted, because it includes you—it is self-knowledge.

Existence is one whole. Everything is included. Yet each thing plays a particular part according to the level of Being, the level of consciousness it has.

We have been given tools we don't know how to use, so we're not in charge of them. One of these tools is our body. One is our mind. One is our feelings. We don't have a high enough level of consciousness to use them correctly.

But it is possible to raise your level of consciousness and bring meaning to your life. To be conscious means to *taste* your existence, moment after moment. When you taste your existence, you find meaning. You become conscious, and the light of consciousness that's within you shines on whatever and whoever you interact with. Your relationship to life becomes harmonious.

*T*aste gives you an inner sense of fulfillment, an inner satisfaction. When you lose connection to taste, you lose that sense. That could remind you that something is missing. It's as though an alarm goes off, and lets you know something is missing.

Say you are sitting by a stream. You can't just say that you and the stream are one, because then that oneness, that unity, is only in your mind. Your Timeless aspect is in unity with that water. But in your manifested aspect, you and the water are not one. You are you, and the water is water. To be real means to be you as a person, without losing connection to your Timeless nature, and to be your Timeless nature without losing your particularity. Existence is not just unmanifested. It is also manifested. Existence is the totality of unmanifested Awareness and manifested Awareness.

The question is not "What do I know?" The question is "Do I *exist*?" Truth is not something you can possess. You can't have the Truth—you can only come to the Moment—to the *experience* of the Truth.

When you *exist*, you don't need ideas about Existence. When you have water, do you need the idea of water? Only when you don't have something, you grab onto the idea of it. When you have it, you don't need ideas.

Allow your body to be here. Know that your body breathes. Nothing extra is needed. Simply sit here, in this atmosphere. There is no need for the past or future. In the present moment, here, in this atmosphere, body breathes. With each inhalation, take in what you need. With each exhalation, let go of what is not needed. Thoughts come and go. Don't resist them, and don't grab onto them. Feelings and sensations arise. Allow them to be. No extra desire is needed. Just being here is sufficient. No need for worry or anxiety. No need to consider how others think of you. We are all in the same boat, existing together in this particular moment. The past is gone. The future is taking care of itself. Your business is this very moment.

There is an aspect of Divine existence within each of us, always and everywhere. We are here to be here. No effort is needed to be. The thought "I am not" is extra.

This moment is. *I exist.* Everything is interconnected and interrelated, therefore, you exist in unity, unseparated—I accept what is, therefore, *I am.* Every condition is temporary—it comes and goes. Your existence is not affected by conditions. It's aware only of the moment. The law of constant change is eternal. There is a joy in the process of inhalation and exhalation when we are with it. Reality is eternal and always present. The unreal appears and disappears, but that which is real is permanent and unchanging, always and everywhere, permanently connected to the creative intelligence of the universe. In the heart, we know it. In the mind, we try to figure it out. The language of the heart is silence. The language of the mind is thought. But there are moments in which the taste of existence unites the heart and mind. Then the mind has Conscious light. Those are the moments in which we realize our true existence. We find our existence in *is-ness*. There is nothing extra. Everything is as it should be. The light of Consciousness gives the texture of reality to everything that exists, and we see things as they are.

here is the past right now? Or the future? Only this moment exists. There is nothing in this moment that's for later. All our possibilities are in this moment.

25

What if you could see that your eyes, ears, hands, feet—every part of your body, and each and every thing that they do—are actually Existence manifesting? Every manifestation of your body is Existence manifesting. It's the same for everyone else! There is *one* life, *one* energy, *one* Consciousness, *one* Awareness. Everything, and every manifestation, comes from the same Source.

To see things as they really are, you have to come back to the Source. You have to look from the Source, from the center, from the taste of your existence.

The Truth *is*. It's not something we come to. It's the *presence* of Existence. The Truth is always present—but we may not know it. You don't have to strive to reach the Truth—you just have to let go of falsity.

At some point in our life, we may become grateful for all the challenges life presents us with, because we know we can use them to purify ourselves and gain a little more inner strength. We wish to realize our potential to be in harmony with the totality of everything that exists.

Existence has two aspects—Absolute (eternal) and relative (temporary). If we remain connected to the eternal aspect while living our life in time, the relative becomes real. Everything becomes meaningful. Meaning isn't in the relative. We have to bring meaning to it. Meaning comes from our True nature, from the Source.

We have to live with the meaninglessness of our life until we see our own nothingness. Then we're ready to ask for help so we can begin to develop. Then the seed inside us can open, and we see that, like other seeds, it has two halves. One part is Consciousness. It's like a light that lets us penetrate the surface of phenomena and see their actual nature. The other part is Conscience. It's the original voice that guides us by showing us how to use our knowledge and transform it into understanding that can support and nurture life.

In our essence, we have a desire for Truth. We have a desire for meaning. We have a desire for purpose. We have a desire for reality. We have the desire to be human. We have the desire to be truly generous and compassionate, instead of just pretending we are that way. The mind only pretends, but in truth, you are that. Because you are Existence. You wish for the welfare of all that exists, because you see there is actually no separation.

Your mind, feelings, and body have something in common—they enjoy the peaceful state of being present whenever that becomes available to them. How can you support that? By having acceptance, by letting them do what they do! Your mind has thoughts. Your emotional center has feelings. Your body moves and receives sensory input. When you stop interfering with these activities, they stop causing you problems, and your mind, feelings, and body are at peace with each other.

Thoughts come to your mind. Don't interfere—let them come, and let them go. They're not even your thoughts! They come from elsewhere. Don't make them your business. Don't identify with them.

You can do the same thing with your feelings and with the sensory input that comes to you. Let that come and go. Then you can see that your mind, feelings, and body are just tools. They're not you.

31

When you are present, and you inhale, Existence is inhaling. When you exhale, Existence is exhaling. As you inhale, you receive from your Timeless nature. When you exhale, you give yourself back to the Source. You come into existence moment after moment.

Being who you really are and being fully present are the same. When you are present, you are yourself.

Allow the body to be relaxed. Allow your thoughts, feelings, and sensations to be as they are, and see that this is just as it is. We are supported by Existence. We are included in Existence—nothing is separate. There is one whole unity. Everything belongs. Time exists only moment by moment. Each moment is new and fresh, as if all and everything was created only then. The heart knows, the mind doesn't. The body is an instrument that has all levels of consciousness, and supports us.

When the need to *know* and the need to *become* are as obvious to us as the needs of the body, we enter the nurturing process of being supported by Existence, moment after moment. "Who are you?" is answered in "you *are*." That means you always have to start by becoming present. Only the present can give life to the past and future, by being time and Timeless simultaneously. The nature of all that exists is light, and so, light is in all things.

In the moment you can truly say "I exist," you are in harmony with yourself, with your surroundings, with all life.

In the Moment, the observable universe and the realizable universe become one. When you *know* you exist, you know what "realizable" means, and you can observe yourself and everything in the observable universe. When you taste the realizable universe, you see things for what they are. You understand that what you observe is, at the same time, part of the realizable universe. So you see things in unity.

That which dies is not you. The body will die. It's not you. Thoughts will die. They're not you. Your feelings will die. They're not you. Your senses will die. They're not you. That which is *conscious* of all those doesn't die. It wasn't born to die! It is ever-present.

The purpose of our life is to know reality. When we know reality, we don't live in the past and future. We are present.

Existence gave you life. How can you pay that back? By living your life and appreciating every moment.

This moment exists. We are *Being*, emanated from our Timeless nature to our relative nature. Absolute nature and relative nature—unseparated. They exist eternally, free from time and space, and yet time and space are part of our relative nature, subject to two great cosmic laws— the great cosmic law of constant change, and the great cosmic law that maintains the harmony of Existence. The cosmic purpose must be fulfilled. The cosmic harmony cannot be disturbed. Therefore, we are as we are, moment after moment.

The relationship between our Timeless nature and our relative nature can be understood in *I am*. The *I*, the direct emanation of our Timeless nature, in the *am-ness* of itself, gives the taste of Existence to our relative nature. To have a proper relationship to everything that exists, we need to have a proper relationship to ourself. Knowing we exist must be present in everything we do. There is one whole, unseparated Existence, one whole, unified, inclusive. Everything, as it is, is part of this dynamic Existence. When we are as we are, we see everything as it really is.

To have a proper dimension of consciousness, so we can go through life and extract benefit for our development, we need to be awake. Being has to participate in our consciousness, so it becomes *Being*-consciousness. Then we see everything is related to our own existence, and we are supported by all that exists. Everything we come in contact with becomes real for us. We know that when we are *awake*.

When you come to the present moment, you have everything you want. When you don't have what you want, it's because you're living in the past or future.

In the real sense, you are a billionaire, but your bank is only open in the moment, not yesterday or tomorrow.

To give something to someone, you have to have something. What is it that you can give? Your presence. Come to your body and be present. Then you have presence.

Whatever question you ask yourself, no matter how great your understanding, and no matter how perfectly you answer, you come to the point where you see that the bottom line is you really *don't* know. Always, there is something greater than your understanding. Reality is always greater than your understanding. So you have to leave room for "I don't know." That's why the only proper position, the only safe position, is to always remain a student.

We live in the passive state. Seeing and accepting bring us out of it. A meaningful aim would be to be in the receptive state, where we are connected to our True nature, and we receive Conscious energy. With the light of Consciousness, we can see things as they are.

But we can't come from the passive state to the receptive state. We first have to come to the active state. We are so far from the receptive state. In the receptive state, we experience the unity of all things. We can come to the active state—by bringing our mind and body together. When they work as a unit, you're in the active state. When they're not working as a unit, you're in the passive state, no matter what you're doing.

So the direction is clear—bring body and mind together. When you do that enough, the receptive state is given to you. It's not achievable. It's receivable.

When our activities are motivated by external influences, we are in the passive state, even when we are doing all kinds of things.

When we make a decision to intentionally participate in what we're doing, we enter the active state.

When our Being participates in what we're doing, we're in the receptive state.

When we're motivated by the desire for Self-understanding, there is no extra in what we're doing.

45

The body can only be experienced in the present. When you relate to how the body was yesterday, or how it will be tomorrow, you're relating only conceptually.

When you *taste* that *body breathes*, you enter into *is-ness*, because taste is in *is-ness*. When you are in it, your temporary aspect is not separated from your eternal aspect, and you can see things as they really are.

Our ego is self-made, created from our thoughts. It becomes our prison of crystallizations, conditioning, and limitations. Our ego thinks small. It's afraid and wants security.

When you raise your level of consciousness, your mind finds actual security. Then it opens. The light of Consciousness enters, and you can think, you can ponder, you can have insights, you can realize. You aren't dependent on outside knowledge. True knowledge exists in the moment, and you *directly* connect to it within yourself.

There's a poem that says:

> We can't take the heat.
>
> We can't take the cold.
>
> We can't take anything!
>
> So why all this puffing ourselves up?

There are two basic forces in the universe. One is Existence as Consciousness, wishing to understand itself through unifying. The other is Existence as Consciousness, wishing to understand itself through diversifying, through manifesting.

Information can be given to us from outside. Knowledge also comes from outside, but you have to put some energy into examining it.

Knowing is different. Part comes from outside and part from inside. When your feelings are touched and take the outside influence in, you have knowing. In knowing, there is both experience and feelings.

Understanding comes from within. It gives you realization of your existence. What is it you understand? Yourself.

Being is yet another level. You experience your existence in the moment, and within that, you have understanding of who you are. That gives you depth.

Then there is will. In order to have real will, you first have to be touched by total understanding of who you are, have a universal direction, and the desire to fulfill the universal need.

Then there is the ability to create. Someone in this level can actualize the universal potential.

Knowledge that comes from Awareness *empties* the mind—it doesn't fill it! Being that comes from Awareness doesn't have a personal character—it is *emptiness.* Love that comes from Awareness doesn't need our superficial feelings to express itself. It's the substance of Awareness itself, and is simply present.

52

Self-understanding means understanding in the moment. The self you need to understand exists in this moment. Being and understanding are one. To understand yourself means to *exist*.

Your instinctive energy comes from the connection between the Earth as your mother, and your body, as her child. When you are connected to your body, you have that energy. It functions without being subject to the mind.

When you try to figure out life with your mind, you become confused. And if you ask your mind to solve your confusion, it writes you a prescription: "You need more thinking."

Your thoughts are like imaginary food. No matter how much you eat, you remain hungry. To receive nourishment, light has to come into your mind. When something touches your Being, a tiny opening appears, and the light of Consciousness can enter. Then the mind is nourished. It turns to face the light and becomes quiet.

55

Your body is an incredible instrument. You can learn a lot from it. But if you take your body to be you, you don't learn anything from it. You can't learn from something you are identified with. Identification actually separates you from what you're identified with.

The child of society, that which we've acquired and has become our personality, has certain characteristics. It lives its life in worry and anxiety and imaginary separation. It has associative thoughts and reactive emotions. It has information, but no wisdom. It has comparative suffering. It suffers by comparing itself to others, and comparing what it has to what others have. The child of society postpones things until later. It wastes time. It's always in a rush. It likes to gossip.

The child of Existence, our essential nature, also has particular characteristics. It is benevolent. It emanates love, aliveness, and meaning. It lives in the present. It doesn't know worry or anxiety. It knows only unity. It has no thoughts, no feelings. It has wisdom, not information. It doesn't see "others" and so, doesn't compare. The child of Existence emanates love and its love grows. Its love is the realization of your existence. The child of Existence is timelessly present in time, and so, doesn't relate to "later." It radiates energy and its inner wealth. It is always still and silent. It never rushes. It never gossips. In fact, it doesn't talk. It emanates.

57

What does it mean to let go of extra? We can't let go of anything, unless we replace it with something else. If you receive the taste of being present, you can let go of extra, because in that taste, you don't need extra. That taste is freedom from what you think you are.

We need to find a bridge, a bridge we can stand on. You acknowledge your particularity, your name and form. At the same time, you see your connection to the Source. You find your own place, your actual place, between your Timeless nature and your time nature, between your observable aspect and realizable aspect, between life and form, between whole and part. In the relationship between the relative and the Absolute, we can understand the creation and maintenance of the world.

What makes you real? You become real when reality looks at you. That means you need your Timeless nature to be participating in your life. Then your relative aspect can manifest without being separated from reality, without being separated from your Timeless nature.

In order to support life, we need to support ourselves. And to support ourselves, we need to become conscious of our existence.

The more you are truly yourself, the more presence
you have.

Your body is real, but only when there is a unified *I* that sees it. Otherwise, what body do you have? Nothing but an idea in your mind. The light of Existence has to shine—it illuminates your *I* and makes it real. The *I* shines light on the body and makes it real, and when you connect to it, you are connected to Existence, because Existence is manifesting in the form of a body.

62

Where are you when you're not present? You can never know. The only possibility of knowing where you are is to be present.

The most profitable journey you can take is the journey from complication towards simplicity, from diversity towards unity. How fast you're traveling is not important. Nor how far you've gone. The important thing is that you're moving in the right direction.

The truth of everything that exists is light, down to the subatomic particles of the universe. When the mind and the heart unite, they create Being-understanding. There, we don't separate ourselves from our Timeless nature. That's what it means to have confidence in your Timeless nature. Your life didn't begin with birth, and doesn't end when your body goes back into the ground. We have to wake up to this truth, so we can rise above the fear of death. Then we may be able to not fear life, because life and death are head and tail of one coin.

There is light, but first you have to receive it in your heart. Then you understand that when you receive the Truth, your body is filled with light. Then the body is a temple of wisdom, whose atoms and molecules are constantly dancing in the temple of Existence. We are created in the image of God. There are currents of energy in the body that can be tasted, but not sensed with our sense organs. That's how magnificent life is. Life is eternal, and everlasting, but manifests moment after moment in time, without losing its Timeless nature. When you experience yourself in the present, you have a chance to know who you really are.

65

Light nurtures light. Being nurtures Being. But the mind only confuses or impresses another mind.

The body is consciousness. And all consciousness is an expression of Awareness. Nothing exists by itself. The body, like everything else, is an expression of the whole, in the whole.

A philosophy may answer your questions. Truth never answers them. Truth opens you up, so your questions become deeper questions. Truth guides you towards finding yourself through raising your level of consciousness. And the finer your consciousness becomes, the more room is created for Truth to be in your life.

To have real feelings, we need to develop. Our ordinary feelings are just reactions to our thoughts. When we raise our level of consciousness above the level of mechanical consciousness, to the level in which we *taste* our existence, we come to the threshold of our real feelings.

We need a new way of thinking, a new way of feeling, a new way of manifesting. We need a new way of relating to life. What's your motivation for saying what you are saying? For doing what you're doing? Seeing your motivation can help bring you to a new way.

When you are grateful, you open up. Life becomes alive for you.

When we let go of thoughts, we come to quiet mind.
When we let go of our feelings, we come to quiet heart.
When the quiet mind and quiet heart come together,
they become a mirror in which we can see our True self.
When we're connected to our essential nature, we have
love for everything we see.

Thoughts can't quiet the mind. You can't put out a fire with fire. Thoughts can't eliminate thoughts. Past and future are the mind's territory. But the body can support us to come to the present. Coming to the body, you come to physical reality. Your senses show you a picture of reality, but *taste* connects you to the reality of the body.

73

When harmony between the mind, feelings, and body is experienced, you experience real health.

If you really look, you'll see that you're ruled by your body. Not your actual body, but by your concepts, your assumptions about it. Your actual body is also life. It's matter, energy, Consciousness, and Awareness. When you connect to your actual body, you are with the reality of yourself.

When you let go of your concepts, you can connect to your actual body.

When you let go of the false, the real shows itself. When you brush the dust off the surface, gold shines.

The purpose of our existence in this body, on this Earth, and the purpose of everything else that exists cannot be separated from the purpose of Existence as a whole. Reality wishes to be known, and so the desire to know yourself is supported by Existence. The process of knowing yourself means raising your level of consciousness. The finer the consciousness, the more we see things as they are.

True knowledge is knowledge of Being. It's in between our Absolute, unchanging aspect and our relative, changing aspect. Moment after moment, we enter into relative existence. Moment after moment, we return to our Absolute aspect. The Absolute and relative aspects are unseparated, and form the dynamic of our universe and our existence. Moment after moment, new universe, new you, new everything.

Nothing is identifiable as a separate thing, because everything is subject to the great cosmic law of constant change. We are light. We come from light. We return to light. Light is the only substance, the building block of the entire universe. To know reality, we need to be real. And to be real, we need to let go of assumptions and concepts.

Do you see how short-sighted it is to expect to understand the whole by examining smaller and smaller parts? First you have to take in the whole, then you can understand the parts. First you have to see the whole body, then you can study organs. First you have to become connected to the Totality, then you can make sense of this universe.

When you *experience* what is in the heart, your words aren't extra. Heart means the knowledge of being in unity.

You are real, but you are not what you imagine yourself to be, because your ideas come from the past, from an imaginarily separated time and place. You are real in the Moment, because that's where all reality is.

79

If you win a billion dollars, the fear of losing it comes with it. But the present moment is beyond time and space, and the joy of being present is free from fear and desire.

Someone asked a wise man, "Does evil exist?"
"Oh yes," he said. "The whole world is filled up with it!"
"And you're not afraid of it?"
"Why should I be?"
"But you said evil is all over."
"Yes, but at the presence of one second of Love, it disappears."

In a moment of connection—in a moment where Love is—evil, fear, negativity, conflict all disappear. That's why you don't need to focus on them, because they aren't real. They appear in the absence of Love. Real love is our intimate connection to the Source.

Look at how dark it is in the middle of the night. What happens if you light one candle? Can the darkness remain in the presence of the candle?

We "experience" darkness in the absence of light. What is your mind doing to you? Always going to the past and future, collecting all the things you've done wrong, all the things you're afraid of. But what do they have to do with you? They are there in the absence of being connected to your body. You should be grateful to them, because they show you you're not connected. When you're looking at them, it means you're not seeing yourself. So you don't need to have negativity towards your unconscious manifestations or those of others—they're there to remind you to come back to yourself.

81

Real understanding is simple. It's in your heart. You don't have to go to your head and search for it.

82

Nothing can be understood in separation. Understanding comes only in unity.

When you look at a flower, how are you looking at it? That depends on how you are at that moment. If you're preoccupied with money you owe, you read this sentence on every petal: "How am I going to pay my bills?"

If you're upset with someone when you listen to the sound of the water flowing in a river, you hear: "He shouldn't have treated me that way!"

A man returned from a hiking trip up in the mountains. "Where have you been?" a friend asked him.

"To the most crowded place on Earth!" he answered. "My own mind."

84

Only Existence exists. If you want to see something else, you have to imagine it.

Something exists that is higher than us. When we fall in love with it, everything we do in life, we do for its sake. And that becomes an inexhaustible source of energy.

Heaven is not "somewhere up there," not a place to go to. It's the present moment.

Moment after moment, we are supported by Existence. The word "after" doesn't refer to time or space. Each moment is within each moment. And all of them are one fundamental unity that harmoniously contains all that exists.

We don't exist separately. Because Awareness is, we are. When we sense and taste the interconnectedness of all that exists, we are *awake*. When we feel separate and identify with ourselves as "me," we are asleep. We awaken from sleep, and then fall asleep again. This process is constant, so waking up is moment after moment. We exist in the dynamic of constant change. Change is part of the timeless nature of Existence, and so, penetrates time. Change is the reality of our existence.

The essential reality of Existence is love. Existence is nothing but love. And your intimate connection to that love is the reality of yourself. That's your heart. The heart is the *is-ness* of life.

Love is the electricity of the universe. And it runs through everything that exists. An atom is held together by the power of love. A blade of grass is related to the whole of Existence through its love for life. Love is the reality of who you are. Everything else is extra.

Real love cannot be turned into anything else. It never becomes hatred or animosity. To really love, you have to *exist*. You need a real *I*. That *I* can love. "You" can't.

Real love is unconditional. That's very big. But we can start with having well-wishing for others. That's something we can do. To have well-wishing, we need to let go of fear. That's why we need to become present. When you are present, you lose your fear, and you experience an inner satisfaction from your well-wishing. That's the beginning of love. When there is love, instead of fear, you experience your connection to everyone and everything.

You *exist*, and thoughts and feelings come and go. As they pass, they change and dissipate. Can you be present and still have thoughts and feelings? Yes. All you need is to not identify with them.

When you are present, you are supported by outer conditions, and by the whole of Existence. You can see what is needed, and you have energy to move in the direction you choose.

Your body is a "form" that presents a picture of reality to you. But the form is made of vibration. Form and its appearance are indicators that there is an underlying reality. If reality wasn't there, there wouldn't be any form, either.

The Absolute sees you as itself, not as something it created. The Absolute *is* you! It's everything that exists. Everything has a Divine nature. When we get caught in appearances and forget the Timeless aspect, there is separation and fear instead of love and unity.

Seeing that you live your life in the absence of Truth is a very big step, one that merits your gratitude.

Our potential is much greater than anything that has ever been written. But first, we have to peel off all the lies. It doesn't matter how little Truth we have. When we have a grain of it, we can enter another dimension of Existence.

Fear of others comes from not being connected to your body. When you're afraid, breathe, and ask your mind just to register your body inhaling and exhaling. When you bring body and mind together, you don't experience fear!

95

Seeing things as they are means seeing them as yourself. It means you see the reality of whatever you're looking at, not its image. It means seeing things with your Being.

"I wish to be present." That's a beautiful aim, provided you couple it with seeing "I am not present." Not being present is not something awful. It's just another event. But if you *experience* that you're not present, it means you have a small degree of presence, otherwise, you wouldn't know you're not present. So you have something to build on, provided you accept what you see.

A student went to his Teacher and said, "Could I be honest?"
The teacher said, "Yes."
The man said, "I'm in love with a girl in my neighborhood."
"That's wonderful. Does she know?"
"Oh no! I never want her to know."
"Why not?"
"Why should I risk destroying something so beautiful, so great, so magnificent?"

Whatever we wish, as long as it remains in our imagination, seems magical. No one can oppose it. There's only one thing wrong with imagination—it doesn't pay off. You can eat all the imaginary bread you want, but your stomach remains empty.

So what should we do? We can't throw imagination away. But by seeing that it's only imagination, we enter into reality. If your aim is to be present, all those times you see you are not present are gifts, provided you accept them as gifts.

Words are man-made. They are not the Truth. But man-made doesn't mean bad. Words can help, but at some point you have to let them go, and come to a direct *experience* of the Truth. Otherwise, you get stuck.

It's said, "If you rely only on God, it brings disaster. If you rely only on yourself, it brings disaster. If you rely on nothing, it brings disaster."

The meaning of our life exists within us. To connect
to it, we need to bring mind, feelings, and body to work
in harmony with each other. When we find the connection between the realizable universe and the observable
universe, we come closer to the taste of our own existence. That which is real is always real and exists within
us. We need to prepare ourselves to be receptive to what
is within, to our True nature, so we can connect to the
meaning and purpose of our life.

The universe is based on the principle of Mutual Support. We are always supported by what we are support-
ing. When we're receptive to our True nature, we receive
what we need in each moment. We are always affected by
what we think, feel, and do. Seeing that, we wish to bring
ourselves to a balanced state before thinking, feeling, or
doing. Then what we do supports life. To support the
body, we need to bring it to a relaxed state. To support
the mind, we need to ask it to think intentionally. And
to support the feelings, we need to bring them to a more
balanced state by having well-wishing.

hat's the purpose of waking up? You wake up in order to have a chance to enter into a greater awakening. It's a process, not a finished product. Otherwise, it would be something "dead," without life. Your body breathes. That's not finished. Because as soon as you're done inhaling, you exhale. When you're done exhaling, you inhale.

A Teacher and a student were standing in an orchard. The Teacher asked, "How many cherries do you think are on that tree?"

"Thousands," the student answered.

"How many of them will become another cherry tree?" the Teacher asked.

"Ten?" the student guessed.

"No. Maybe only one or two," the Teacher said, and then asked, "What do you think will happen to the rest of them?"

"They go to waste," the student said.

"No," the Teacher said. "Nothing in the universe ever goes to waste. Those cherries go back to the soil and nurture the tree."

You are part of Existence whether you know it or not. If you wish to know that, there is a payment to be paid. As soon as you want to know, you find out you are in a level of consciousness that doesn't allow you to know. So you need to raise your level of consciousness, by bringing your Being to participate in your life. Your body is the gift you've been given. It can teach you something that you can't learn any other way—to recognize the present moment by *taste*.

Those who don't have to use all their life energy exclusively for securing their next meal are very fortunate. Many, many people are not in that position. One way those whose lives afford them the time and possibility to invest in their inner life, in their development, can support those who can't do that, is by being sincere in their desire to understand. When you come to balance and harmony in yourself, others are affected, too. The search for the Truth is the most unselfish activity you can have. When you're after the Truth, after understanding, you support life.

The ultimate aim is to become who you really are. The God you know by becoming who you really are is real.

Say you want to help someone, but can't find a way to. You can at least picture yourself in their shoes. That's a good beginning.

Cleansing your emotions means seeing for yourself, understanding for yourself, that there is no benefit whatsoever in disliking or hating someone. No one else is responsible for your reactions. You are!

When you are bothered by someone, you need to have well-wishing for them. Ask for blessings for them. Wish them well. This is how you cleanse your emotions.

Complication takes you toward negativity. Simplicity brings you toward compassion. In every moment, there is one small step we can take, and we need to be grateful when we take it. That is the way of actualizing.

The finer our consciousness, the closer we are to the Source, the more we attract conditions to our life that support our growth.

Evolution must continue, so humanity has a purpose to fulfill—to support each other in the evolution of our consciousness. That's what creates a real bond, an essential bond between us. Only by giving can you actually receive. This is the Law of the Universe. But so few of us understand this.

The desire to be special can interfere with self-development. "Extra" is whatever is in the way of harmony. If you are "you," you become extra, because extra means whatever is separate from unity.

We need to have the posture of the person who wishes to support the Truth, to support what is good, real, alive. The more we have that posture, the more able we are to take a step towards a constructive life and away from a destructive one. These are the times in which you have to rise above animosity and negativity, first of all, towards your friends and family. Make contact. Let go, so they can let go. You can reunite with all those whom you once appreciated, and re-establish friendship. Nothing comes from hatred and animosity, but to have well-wishing for many people, to be surrounded by people you love and respect makes you stronger, so you are more able to help.

There is enough energy available in these times to invest constructively in the world. So clean your house. Put things in order in your life. Organize yourself mentally, physically, and emotionally, so you can maybe help your friends and neighbors as well. Be open to appreciate others, to appreciate life. Sometimes events show us how precious life is, and how important it is to be alive. Through that appreciation, we should respect others and keep a posture of well-wishing all the way through life.

Do the things you've postponed for years. There is enough energy, if you roll up your sleeves. There is a lot of energy available to do things right. That's the way to use negative energy and transform it into something constructive and positive. Start at home, with yourself. Instead of getting caught in the useless chit-chat of the mind, clean up your surroundings. Organize your life, because you are going to need an organized life to deal with all the things that come up.

If we accustom ourselves to have well-wishing for everyone and everything around us, we will grow.

The true meaning of compassion is to receive someone as yourself. That's the highest form of compassion. Before we come to that level, we may be able to relate to anyone we come in contact with without judgment. Even before that, you could know, even if it's mental knowing, that you have life, and the people around you have life. On the day-to-day level, do what you can, simply, fully, and joyfully. That's how you begin to express your compassion.

114

Development means becoming able to manifest from the level of consciousness that is needed.

A poet had a friend. Something happened between them that made them very distant. During that period, the poet suffered a lot, because he loved his friend deeply. Finally, he wrote him a letter: "Dear friend, come back and let's appreciate each other, because soon this body will disappear. Negative thinking creates a cloud in our relationship. Let it go. Come to the sunshine. I'm sure that when I die, you will come and kiss my grave. Why not be with me now?"

Giving relationships your best opens the possibility for them to become more essential. Relating to the other person as an aspect of yourself, as yourself in the form of the other person, you can discover that they are here to teach you to relate to yourself. That's the purpose of relationships. Ask yourself, "What is it I could learn from this?" Then you end up being grateful to the other person regardless of how they behave. This is the remedy we all need to use, because planet Earth is a tough planet. It's a school, and the purpose of a school is to place difficulties in front of you. Then you have to learn how to benefit from them.

Being *awake* means experiencing that nothing is separate from you. That which is awake is also total.

The Truth can't be poured into a mold. In fact, Truth breaks the mold!

What is the sun? Your Timeless nature. What blocks its light? Your thoughts. They create a shadow and you think that shadow is you!

There is a beautiful story. A student was walking by a lake and suddenly heard someone call his name. He looked and saw a fish with its head out of the water calling, "Hey, hey, hey!"

"What is it?" asked the student.

"I'm thirsty!" the fish said.

"How is that possible?" the student asked. "How could you be in this lake and say you are thirsty?"

"How is it possible," said the fish, "that you are surrounded by life, but are searching for God?"

The world doesn't need your criticism—it needs healing. The worst person doesn't need to be criticized, because their behavior comes from a lack of understanding. They need to be healed—to become whole, to become healthy in the true sense.

121

Knowing and Being are not two things. They are one. When you *are*, you *know*. When you *know*, you *are*.

122

When you let go of all extra, you and reality become one.

When your mind talks, you end up dissatisfied. But when your Being participates, communicating helps raise your level of consciousness. You experience satisfaction from speaking—essential satisfaction.

Someone went to a Teacher and said, "I have trouble communicating with people."

"It's really very simple," the Teacher told him. "You just have to practice listening."

125

Consciousness has two aspects—the desire to really see how you manifest in the given conditions of your life, and the desire for what you say and do to have a beneficial effect on others.

Awareness gives life. Consciousness can create form, but it cannot give life to form. So to be alive in the true sense of the word is to be connected directly to the Source. To do that, we need finer consciousness.

When Existence exists for you, when you *know* Existence exists, your thoughts are real. But the reality of Existence is not dependent on thought.

Every single thing you've gone through in your life up to this moment was necessary. But that doesn't mean you have to repeat any of it!

In the orchard of Existence, you are free to pick any fruit you like.

The more extra you have, the less ability to see the sun, because extra is like a thick fog. Development really means letting go of extra.

131

Suffering and misery are caused by a lack of understanding. What you understand doesn't bring you suffering. It brings you freedom.

A yellow sparrow and a gray sparrow went to a Master, and the yellow one said, "I can't get my friend to recognize that humans are dangerous, and we should avoid all contact with them. They just want to catch us and make soup out of us."

The gray one said, "If we avoid them, they won't learn from us, and that's our purpose—to teach them to be gentle."

They argued back and forth. Finally, the Master said, "Humans are dangerous—that's true. They each have a positive and a negative side. Your job is to help their positive side become stronger, so they'll be attracted by your sweetness and song. But even then, you have to be careful around them!"

133

The mind is a reasoning tool, but it cannot produce understanding. For understanding, Being is needed.

A man went to a wise man and said, "I have this burning question. Tell me please, what is love?"

The wise man said, "I do not know what love is, but I'll tell you what it's not. Love is not an idea."

You have to make yourself palatable to Existence, so Existence can "eat" you and transform you into itself, into Existence! Palatable means no trace of ego.

I t's easy to sense and feel the existence of God, because God is very near you. You can do that by knowing *I exist, I am here*. When that is true, God is here, because you and God are never separated. You never have been and never will be. There is one Existence, one energy, one Consciousness, one life.

Allow other dimensions of yourself to be available to you, because you have them. There are many dimensions of your essential nature to be reached towards, to awaken to, to be receptive to, so they can give you a different perspective of what life is all about. You need open-heartedness and an open mind to receive consciousness. Moment after moment, we enter into life.

We are asleep, and we need to wake up. Being asleep means living only in the dimension of our sense organs. Awakening means coming to the dimension in which we rely on our consciousness more than our senses.

Someone may have insulted you, but you are the one who let that insult bother you.

It's said that your tongue is something that can make your life heaven or hell.

When well-wishing replaces criticism, you have much more energy to invest in what's needed.

When you are facing the light, and it shines through your consciousness, your thoughts are real. When you turn away from the light, what you see is an assumption, and so are you.

There is no way to understand a God who you take to be separate from you. In separation, unity disappears. When unity disappears, you may say, "God, please…" but you're not giving God room to manifest in your life, because God only manifests in unity.

There's a poem that says:

> Our life is like snow.
>
> Existence is like the hot summer sun.
>
> We see that the snow is melting,
>
> And *still*, we don't feel it's time to wake up!

The question is not "Who is God?" The important thing to ask yourself is "Am I experiencing that God is present?"

Wherever you find Truth, there is Love. Wherever Truth is, Love is.

In the Timeless dimension of the heart, there is Love.

In the Timeless dimension of the mind, there is Consciousness.

Only when the heart and mind unite is there Awareness.

Reality *is*, but you have to invite it into your life. For that, you need receptivity.

We are blessed by life.

We are blessed by what we are,

by knowing *Existence exists*,

by knowing there is perfect harmony in this apparently chaotic world.

We are blessed by knowing we can breathe,

by knowing we can call a friend,

by knowing we can support life in whatever small way we are able.

The mind can be impressed, but the heart will only settle for Truth.

They asked a wise man, "What is the nature of reality?"

He answered, "Open yourself up, and there is no closed door in the entire Existence."

We have the possibility to be in harmony with all that exists. Our responsibility is to work towards unifying ourselves.

Let the beauty of life touch your heart. And then, with that heart, touch the universe. Let the universe that your heart touched become your pillow when you sleep at night.

Be well!

The grace of Existence is ever-present,

and it's the entirety.

It lights up

and gives life to the world.

Moment by moment, it shines.

BREEMA

Being

Right now

Everywhere

Every moment

Myself

Actually

The Breema Center

Since 1980, the Breema Center has been presenting Breema's practical approach to harmony and Self-understanding. The world headquarters for practitioner and instructor certification and continuing education, the Center also gives classes, workshops, and intensives for beginning, intermediate, and advanced students. People come from all over the world, attracted by Breema's philosophy, principles, bodywork, and exercises. Studying at the Center, they find essential support in creating a new, unified relationship between the body, mind, and feelings, and in bringing greater harmony and presence to their lives.

The Breema Center maintains an active relationship with certified practitioners and instructors, and an up-to-date international directory of instructors and practitioners, plus listings of Breema classes and presentations worldwide. Information is available on our website, by phone, or mail.

THE BREEMA CENTER
Jon Schreiber, D.C., Director
6076 Claremont Avenue
Oakland, CA 94618

510-428-0937
email: center@breema.com
website: breema.com

The Breema Clinic

We have been using Breema bodywork, Self-Breema exercises, and working with the principles of Breema since 1981 to support people to experience greater well-being, harmony, and essential interest in life. Receiving Breema and practicing Self-Breema support the unification of body, mind, and feelings. As these three come together, they begin to function naturally, and we become receptive to finer consciousness. This becomes our entry to real health, which means harmony with Existence.

THE BREEMA CLINIC
Jon Schreiber, D.C., Director
6201 Florio Street
Oakland, CA 94618

510-428-1234
email: clinic@breema.com
website: www.breemahealth.com

Jon Schreiber

Jon Schreiber is the director of the Breema Center, which presents the transformational tools of Breema, Self-Breema, and the Nine Principles of Harmony. He is also the founder and director of the Breema Clinic, which supports people to move in the direction of real health. Since 1980 he has been teaching at the Breema Center, as well as nationally and internationally, and is the author of many books on the philosophy, principles, and practice of Breema.

Books from The Breema Center
in print, eBook, & audio CD format
Available from local and online bookstores

Freedom Comes from Understanding:
Insights for Meaningful Life
— by Jon Schreiber

How does Existence support you? By letting you know you belong. When you become conscious of your own existence, that Consciousness is the beginning of connection to your Timeless nature.

available in print, audio, and eBook
print: hardcover, 172 pages, 5″ x 7.25″ • $18
audio: 2-CD set, read by Jon Schreiber • $20

BREEMA *and the Nine Principles of Harmony*
— by Jon Schreiber

Breema is universal and has great potential value to anyone with a sincere interest in Truth, because it's a practical road to Self-understanding. Breema's timeless principles are applicable to every situation in life, and they open us to the possibility of awakening to the essential unity of Existence in this very moment.

available in print, audio, and eBook
print: hardcover, 168 pages, 7″ x 9″, 81 photos • $25
audio: 2-CD set, read by Jon Schreiber • $20

The Four Relationships *and Other Essential Insights*
— by Jon Schreiber

The Four Relationships—our relationship to the body, our relationship to the outside world, our relationship to ourself, and our relationship to our True nature—provide a universal framework that enables us to usefully relate to the ingredients and issues of our life, and to find a meaningful posture and approach to the questions life places in front of us. This book explores the principles and philosophy of Breema.

available in print, audio, and eBook
print: hardcover, 160 pages, 5″ x 7.25″ • $18
audio: 2-CD set, read by Jon Schreiber • $20

Waking Up to This Moment:
The Essential Meaning of Breema
— by Jon Schreiber

To the extent you are available at this moment, you are doing Breema. It's as simple as that. If you keep this direction clear for yourself and always work with it, you can come to a taste—the taste of being present. Instead of being drawn to the past or future, where you have been conditioned to live, it's possible to live your life with meaning and purpose in the present.

available in print (English & Spanish) and audio (English)
print: hardcover, 168 pages, 7" x 9", 60 color photos • $25
audio: 2-CD set, read by Jon Schreiber • $20

Child of Existence, Child of Society
— by Jon Schreiber

There are two parts of us—the child of Existence and the child of society. The child of society is our acquired aspect, acquired from our education, from books, movies, radio, television, newspapers, the Internet. But we're more than that. We have also been given something by Existence. The child of Existence is our essential aspect, what we are in reality. The aim is to move from this outer part, this acquired part, towards the inner part—to find this essential part of ourself.

available in print, audio, and eBook
print: hardcover, 208 pages, 5" x 7.25" • $18
audio: 2-CD set, read by Jon Schreiber • $20

Your Home Is the Entire Cosmos: *The Wisdom of Breema*
— by Jon Schreiber

The desire to know, to be, and to understand is the essential heritage of being human. The most meaningful aspect of that desire is the desire to know oneself, to be oneself, and to understand oneself. Even though we don't know what "self" means, this gives us direction. It points towards you. In order to develop, you need to know yourself. To the extent you know yourself, you know other things, too.

print: hardcover, 192 pages, 5" x 7.25" • $18

Coming to Yourself: *The Art of Practicing Breema*
— by Jon Schreiber

To see things as they are, we have to *be* as we are. The taste of Being is received in the absence of thoughts, feelings, and sensations. When we receive that taste, we can see thoughts as thoughts, feelings as feelings, sensations as sensations. By not identifying with them, we enter into the awareness of our existence.

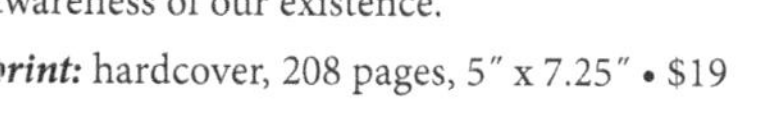

print: hardcover, 208 pages, 5" x 7.25" • $19

Seeing Things As They Really Are
— by Jon Schreiber

You can only see things as they really are when you see yourself as you are in relation to them. It means to see things as a part of your existence, not as separate phenomena. Existence is one unified whole—nothing separate exists. There is one life force, and it enters into everything that has been created. That means it also flows through you. When you are present, you experience it.

available in print, audio, and eBook
print: hardcover, 192 pages, 5" x 7.25" • $19

The Taste of Being Present: *Essential Wisdom of Breema*
— by Jon Schreiber

You have to know where you are, wherever you are. Establish one "marker"—I am here in this moment. This first step is the most important thing in the world! Wherever you are, be where you are. Then, you can see the next step. You study Breema in order to study yourself. You do Breema in order to be yourself. Being yourself means body, mind, and feelings functioning in the receptive state, receiving Conscious energy from your True nature. In those moments, you know yourself.

available in print, audio, and eBook
print: hardcover, 172 pages, 5" x 7.25" • $18
audio: 2-CD set, read by Jon Schreiber • $20

Walking into the Sun:
Stories from Classes at the Breema Center
— collected by Jon Schreiber

A collection of teaching stories from early Breema classes that brings the philosophy and principles of Breema to life. Traditional parables, modern anecdotes, and both old and newer proverbs and sayings help awaken our desire for a more meaningful life.

available in print and eBook
print: hardcover, 132 pages, 5.5" x 8.5" • $22.95

Knowing and Being: *Breema and the Meaning of Your Life*
— by Jon Schreiber

All moments of life are blessings if we are present. We have to clearly see that the past is gone and the future is "elsewhere." But in this moment, we could be here, present. If there's something you need to do to repair the past, you still have to do it in this moment. In the present, there's always a chance to take a correct step for your life. If you need to prepare for the future, you can only do it in the present. That's where all your possibilities are.

available in print and eBook
print: hardcover, 168 pages, 5.5" x 8.5" • $18

First You Have to *Be:*
The Nine Principles of Harmony in Breema and Life
— by Jon Schreiber

The purpose of Breema bodywork, Self-Breema exercises, and Breema's philosophy is to show us a new way of life—the way to be yourself in life, the way to participate in life, not in the reactive state, but in the active state, with body and mind together. From there, you have a chance to come to the receptive state—body, mind, and feelings together.

available in print and audio
print: hardcover, 192 pages, 5″ x 7.25″ • $18
audio: 2-CD set, read by Jon Schreiber • $20

Real Health Means Harmony with Existence:
The Art of Practicing Breema
— by Jon Schreiber

You do Breema in order to become present, and by remaining present, to have presence, which is to receive the emanation of what *is*. In that, your *Being* participates. Understanding is a property of Being, and Being is in harmony with what is.

available in print and eBook
print: hardcover, 208 pages, 5″ x 7.25″ • $18

Every Moment Is Eternal: *The Timeless Wisdom of Breema*
— by Jon Schreiber

This book talks to our essential nature, because Truth already exists there. The more our essence is nurtured, the greater the chance that cracks may appear in our conditioned attitude towards life. Through these cracks, we may see things we haven't seen before, and nourish our essential desire for Self-understanding.

available in print and eBook
print: hardcover, 208 pages, 4.5″ x 6″ • $15

Freedom Is in This Moment: *365 Insights for Daily Life*
— by Jon Schreiber

When you read these writings, you are filled up with an inner resonance, because their reality and meaning are in you as well as all around you. When you hear the Truth, you also hear it inside of yourself, in your very essence. The Truth is not something foreign. It's already part of you just because you exist!

available in print and eBook
print: hardcover, 448 pages, 4.5″ x 6″ • $18.95

In the Heart of the Moment: *Essential Poetry*
— collected by Jon Schreiber

These poems are doorways that open into the heart of Breema as a teaching for Self-understanding, and for understanding the world and our place and purpose in it.

print: hardcover, 112 pages, 5.25″ x 8″ • $15

In the Garden of All Possibilities: *Essential Poetry*
— collected by Jon Schreiber

These poems are meant to harmonize our inner aspect and bring it into equilibrium with Existence. Their vibration and sequence create a meaning. When you listen, you become an instrument. The poems tune you, and you resonate with their music.

print: hardcover, 112 pages, 5.25″ x 8″ • $15

Call **510.428.0937** to order **Breema Center books & CDs,**
or see our Bookstore at: **www.breema.com**
Check your favorite online stores for our eBooks.